Little Lambs

PAUL

by Karen Williamson
Illustrated by Sarah Conner

CANDLE
BOOKS

In Jerusalem there lived a man named Paul.
He hated people who loved Jesus.

He hunted them down and threw them in jail.

One day Paul set out for the city of Damascus. He wanted to arrest people there who loved Jesus.

On the road, a bright light suddenly blinded him.

The voice of Jesus asked him,
"Paul, *why* are you hurting my people?"

Paul continued on his way to Damascus.
There, God gave him back his sight.

But Paul was a changed man.
Now he *loved* Jesus and wanted
to tell others about him.

Meanwhile, enemies were plotting to kill Paul.

One dark night, some friends helped him escape the city. They let him down from the wall in a basket.

"I must tell people in other countries about the love of Jesus," Paul decided.

So he sailed off with his good friend, Barnabas.

They visited many towns, telling people Jesus had risen from the dead.

Some people believed
and became Christians.

Others got angry and hurt Paul
and Barnabas.

Paul visited the city of Jerusalem.
There enemies captured him.

He was put on trial,
and kept in prison
for two years.

Then they sent him by ship
to the city of Rome, to be judged.

They soon sailed into a fierce storm.
"*We're all going to drown!*" yelled the sailors.

"God has promised *everyone* will be safe," Paul told them.

The storm grew worse and worse.
Finally the ship was wrecked on an island.

But, sure enough, they all landed safely.
God protected everybody on Paul's ship!

So Paul arrived at the great city of Rome.
There he was put in prison again.

But even in jail, Paul wrote letters to friends, telling them of the love of Jesus.